A souvenir guide

Powis Castle

Powys

Andrew Barber

Ymddiriedolaeth Genedlaethol
National Trust

The Significance of Powis

The important thing about Powis Castle is that it is a *real* castle. It suffered battle and siege throughout the medieval period, to emerge into the modern age as a comfortable aristocratic residence.

It was burnt and rebuilt on several occasions, the last of which saw its western gates blown up by Parliamentary forces in the Civil War and the castle ransacked. Unlike so many so-called castles in the roll of British country houses, Powis has known the tramp of military feet, the starvation of long siege and the blood-chilling cry of battle.

However, all of this is far back in the history of this grand red castle – the Castell Coch – of the Princes of Powys. Then it was a stronghold to be fought over, now it is a noble family home housing not one, but two of the greatest collections of any country house in the British Isles. How this transformation was achieved is the main story of this guide. It features Welsh princes and Shropshire gentry, a dodgy ducal title and a thrice-created earldom, vast Indian wealth and aristocratic penury, addiction, attainder and wicked uncles. Collections of paintings, sculpture, furniture and much else besides, including trophies from the brutal victory at Seringapatam, will be discussed while the gradual evolution of Powis Castle itself will be charted.

The horticulture of the celebrated terraced gardens and of the magnificent park with its ancient oaks are the subject of a separate publication.

'Wales has a number of medieval castles which developed from fortified strongholds into residencies of considerable opulence and splendour … the two outstanding examples are Powis and Chirk …'

Lindsay Evans,
The Castles of Wales, 1998

What's in a name?
The ancient principality of Powys and its principal family always spelt the name with a 'y'. It is the anglicisation of the name that has caused an 'i' to be substituted for the 'y'. In the telling of this history, the castle itself and the various titles borne by the Herbert and Clive families take the English version of the name (as they ever have done), reserving the historic spelling for the ancient, the romantic and the thoroughly modern parts of the story.

Medieval Powis

'… and the mountains that rise like a rampart all around add a magnificence and grandeur to the scene without giving you any horrid or dreadful ideas …'

A tour into North Wales by Sir George Lyttleton, July 1755

In the 12th and 13th centuries Wales consisted of several independent principalities; the foremost were Gwynedd, Deheubarth and Powys. Strife between them was equal to, if not greater than, battling against the English.

So it was with the first prince to hold a castle in this vicinity, Owain Cyfeiliog, the poet prince who battled with his neighbours but saw his castle lost to an English army under the command of the Archbishop of Canterbury in 1196. It was his son Gwenwynwyn who, on succeeding his father (who had retired to a monastery), re-took the castle the following year. Buoyed by his success and in a brief bid for supremacy amongst the principalities of Wales, Gwenwynwyn gathered all his allies for a great raid into England but, suffering a humiliating defeat in 1198, any hopes of Powys holding sway as primary principality were lost for ever.

In 1208, Gwenwynwyn was summoned to Shrewsbury by King John, stripped of his princely status and forced to accept English overlordship. Worse was to follow as Powys was overrun by the neighbouring principality of Gwynedd and ruled from the north for a generation. Gwenwynwyn's heir, Gruffudd, only succeeded to the government of the principality in 1241, 25 years after his father's death. Initially under the protection of Henry III, Gruffudd defected to Llywelyn ap Gruffudd of Gwynedd after Henry's defeat by Simon de Montfort, Llywelyn's ally, at the Battle of Lewes

Left King John, from a vellum document of 1250–9

Below A marginal drawing of Llywelyn ap Gruffudd (known as Llywelyn the Last), Prince of Wales, who was killed by Adam de Frankton in Wales in 1282, from the 14th-century 'Chronica Roffense' by Matthew Paris

Which castle?

In all of these burnings and resurrections, it is difficult to say which castle was in contention at any one time. Two further sites of potential castles have been identified: one in the deer park and another by the railway station in Welshpool. Neither of these seems to have supported stone structures, whilst the current castle site did. Traces of late 12th-century masonry are discernible at the western end of the south front – are these remnants of the castle burnt by Llywelyn? If so, they are rivalled in antiquity only by parts of the base of the east gateway tower and the south-eastern corner of the south front, both of which hold evidence of very early construction.

in 1264. He then plotted against his new overlord, preparing the 'castle of Pola' for war in 1274 but to no avail as Llywelyn burnt it to the ground. Gruffudd fled to England, and was restored to his lands by Edward I after the final defeat of Llywelyn in 1282. By 1286 a rebuilt castle was in existence, to be listed amongst the possessions of Gruffudd on his death.

Powis Castle sits on a spit of rock which gives it a naturally defensive position, but which also dictates its eccentric form. The ridge provides the material from which the castle is built, the distinctive 'dusky red stone' so often commented upon by travellers and visitors since, although it is the prominent red mortar rather than the stone that actually determines the dominant colour. Its position is also responsible for its defensive aspects, glaring at the approaching English shires to the south and east while presenting a deep ditch and ramparts to the marauding Welsh from the north and west.

Top The castle from the south, with the Outer Gate and Ballroom wing to its left

Above The west-side Outer Gate with wicket door for pedestrian access

Left The Battle of Evesham on 4 August 1265 when Simon de Monfort was killed. The battle was the decisive victory in the Barons' War. From 'Chronica Roffense' by Matthew Paris

The castle

Owain ap Gruffudd ap Gwenwynwyn succeeded his duplicitous father in 1286. As a result of Edward I's crushing victory over Llywelyn – a campaign in which Owain's father had ensured he was on the winning side – when the king summoned a parliament it was as Baron de la Pole that Owain paid homage; he was to be the last Prince of Powys.

Owain died young in 1293, survived by a two-year-old son and a daughter. Owain's mother controlled the lordship during her grandson Gruffudd's minority. Gruffudd succeeded at 17 in 1308 but died a year later, to be succeeded by his 19-year-old sister, Hawise in 1309. She decided to throw in her lot with the English throne and married, immediately on her brother's death, a Shropshire knight, Sir John Charlton who was described as a 'dear servant' of Edward II. Her succession was disputed by her uncles who besieged the castle in 1312. The castle survived the siege as did its doughty mistress, who earned the soubriquet *Gadarn* 'the hardy'. Ennobled as Lord de Charlton of Powys after the relief of the castle and the lifting of the siege, Sir John took his place amongst the powerful Marcher Lords of the border country between England and Wales. Hawises's right to Powis was confirmed by royal charter, and a period of

Left The long approach to the east door, the principal entrance until the transformations of the 1st and 2nd marquesses moved it to the west

comparative peace, punctuated by continuing incursions from Hawises's disgruntled uncle, gave Sir John and Hawise the opportunity to rebuild the castle, giving it much of the general outline and form that it retains today.

Nevertheless, Powis has an odd shape for a medieval castle. Most castles of the Edwardian age consist of a regular defensive keep with towers surrounded by curtain walls punctuated by more towers, then a bailey, ditches and ramparts. In contrast, Powis, although containing all these elements, has them jumbled together in an oddly squeezed arrangement. Constrained by the narrow site, the defensive keep, recognisable by its twin rounded towers at the western gate and the single great tower to the east, is of an elongated shape like a gigantic pair of dividers, while the curtain walls of the bailey extend from each end of the keep.

A range in the western outer court, standing against the north wall, appears to be of the later 16th- or early 17th-century, and the outer curtain wall, with its defensive D-shaped tower, also dates from this time. Bearing in mind the comparatively small proportions of the central keep, it is likely that lean-to timber-framed buildings within the court would have provided the necessary accommodation for a medieval household. Massive towers defended the west gate but these were victims of the Welch Pool Committee after the Civil War (see page 13).

The primary approach to the keep throughout much of the castle's history has been from the east, leading to the defensive focus of the front in the central massive tower, which was given even greater height during Regency improvements. This is approached up a steep slope (only made slightly more accessible by the provision of a long flight of steps in the 17th century) through a series of enclosures, the outer one formerly guarded by a pair of great towers (victims of the Civil War).

The small central courtyard of the keep would have been slightly more spacious, with the lodgings of John and Hawise's castle ranged around the outer walls. A great hall probably stood in the area now occupied by the State Dining Room. The gracious Elizabethan arcade supporting the Long Gallery was a later improvement. The vaulting of the entrance doorway from the west court, separating the two round towers, is one of the few architectural details from the medieval period that remains visible today.

'... upon a majestic Eminence POWIS CASTLE rears its lofty Towers ...'

Sir John Cullum, *Journal of a Tour by Rev. Sir John Cullum through Several Counties of England and Part of North Wales 1774–1775*

Left Pencil drawing of the east entrance, dated 1908

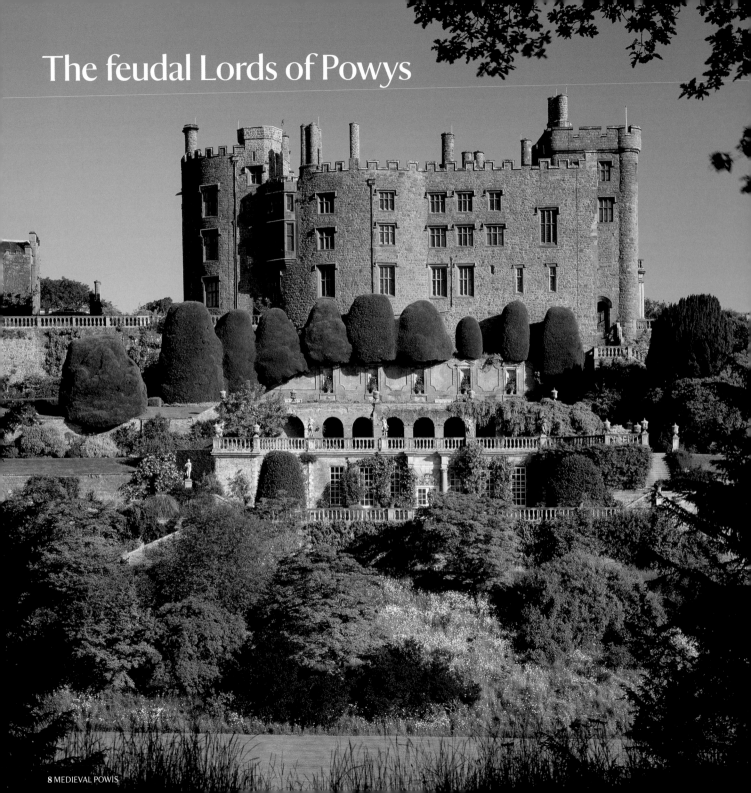

The feudal Lords of Powys

The de Cherleton lords of Powys served their king more or less faithfully for the next century or so. The last, Edward, 5th Baron Charlton, held the castle for the king during the rebellion of Owain Glyndŵr in 1400. At Edward's death in 1421 his co-heirs were two daughters, Joan and Joyce. The estates were split between the two women and their respective husbands, Sir John Grey and Sir John Tiptoft.

For a time, not only were the lands divided, but the castle itself was split between the two families; John Leland the chronicler recorded in 1530 that: 'It hath ii [2] seperatid Wardes whereof the one was the Lord Duddeleys [Joyce's great grandson]. Now both belong to the Lord Powys… The Lord Duddeley's Parte is almost fallen doone. The Lord Powys Parte is meatly good…'.

The Grey interest prevailed, and Sir John and Lady Joan's descendant, Sir Edward Grey, 1st Baron Grey of Powis, had acquired the undivided castle by the 1530s. An inventory taken on Sir Edward's death in 1551 not only gives a picture of how the castle was furnished, but also shows that building work had been taking place to make good the dilapidations.

Identifying which work belongs to Sir Edward and which to his prolific successor, Sir Edward Herbert, is challenging. H. Avray Tipping, writing in *Country Life* in 1917 suggested that the early Renaissance style of the vaulting in the east porch may be Sir Edward Grey's work. The inventory certainly suggests his efforts were concentrated in the keep where a 'new chamber over ye garden' and a 'new gallery' feature. If the latter refers to the Long Gallery, it must have been rebuilt afterwards by Sir Edward Herbert as its architectural style now places it firmly in the later part of the 16th century.

This is not impossible because timber-framed improvements to stone buildings were not unusual, as at Haddon Hall in Derbyshire, only to be replaced in stone by later generations.

A similar story might explain Sir Edward's apparent inaction in the west court where Leland lamented the ruinous state of the castle. It would seem strange if he had done nothing to improve the state of the buildings. He may have built a timber-framed structure where the Ballroom range now stands, only for it to undergo a similar transformation to his improvements elsewhere, since the current range built against the outer wall seems to date from the Elizabethan period. Lack of documentary evidence makes certainty impossible.

Sir Edward Grey died without legitimate heirs and was the last feudal Lord of Powys. He was succeeded by one of his numerous progeny of bastard sons who sold the castle to Sir Edward Herbert, the younger son of the Earl of Pembroke, in 1587.

'they had paintings and tapestries … and tables, cupboards and chairs; their fixed seats were set with cushions of cloth of gold and there were musical instruments …'

Anon. quoting Sir Edward Grey's inventory of 1551 in *Country Life*, May 1908

Opposite The south front and terraces

Below Powis Castle in 1795, from a print by J. ingleby

New owners

Below Edward Herbert, created Lord Herbert of Cherbury in 1629; bronze bust of 1631 by Hubert Le Sueur who had introduced the art of bronze sculpture to Britain in 1625

In acquiring the Powis estate, Sir Edward Herbert was consolidating family dominance in the area, with kinsmen already established in Montgomery and Raglan castles and at Lymore. His father had been created Earl of Pembroke by Edward VI, and descendants of his elder brother still live in the family seat at Wilton in Wiltshire.

Sir Edward spent the last eight years of his life beautifying and enhancing Powis. It is probable that he built the lodging range against the north wall of the west court which now contains the Ballroom and Clive Museum, but later alterations have obscured all Elizabethan work. He altered the inner court, carrying his first-floor Long Gallery on an elegant arcade which was later imitated in the grand portal to the east gate.

Inside he decorated most of the principal spaces in the keep, bringing the interiors up to date with fashionable plaster ceilings and panelling. There are tantalising descriptions of these long-gone Elizabethan decorations by later travellers. John Loveday, visiting in 1732, remarked: 'here are some excellently good fret-work Cielings. particularly One representing ye Zodiac.' A few years later, the antiquarian Thomas Pennant noted that 'the ceiling…is stuccoed with most ridiculous paintings of the zodiac.' The transformations of the 1st and 2nd Marquesses a century later destroyed much of the Elizabethan interior of the castle, but fortunately one significant Elizabethan interior survived: the Long Gallery which Sir Edward completed in 1593.

The Long Gallery

Long galleries were a standard component of Elizabethan suites of state rooms; fine examples survive at Hardwick and Haddon halls in Derbyshire. They provided a space for indoor recreation in bad weather, a place to display both wealth and taste in furnishings, and political allegiances in portraiture. Their plan provided opportunities both for formal entertainment in large numbers and for intimate conversation in the bay windows and embrasures. At Powis, the unique T-shape of the room gave ample opportunity for both.

With the exception of the windows, which have been altered on several occasions, this room retains nearly all its Elizabethan decoration. Fine plasterwork enriches the

'Next is a long narrow gallery, filled with bad portraits'

Thomas Pennant, *A tour in Wales*, 1778

Left The set of twelve marble busts of the Caesars may be the 'twelve statues' brought from London in 1704, but were certainly acquired in Italy earlier than that

Below Also in the Long Gallery is the crouching cat, a gift from the 1st Lord Clive to his wife. The 18th-century marble sculpture cost Clive dear but, as he reported to her, 'I will leave orders … to purchase the Cat … *Coute qui coute* [whatever the cost]'

ceiling with a repeating lobed pattern of interlacing frets, enclosing applied work of fruiting and flowering boughs, and a frieze around the room records family ancestry in colourful heraldic shields. Sir Edward's arms in the fireplace overmantel in the main gallery are flanked by a depiction of Adam and Eve and Lileth the tempting snake. The *trompe l'oeil* panelling may date from a decade or so after Sir Edward's initial work, but it is very much in the late Elizabethan and Jacobean taste, using illusionistic techniques to create a perception of perspective. The ultimate achievement in this form is the gigantic doorway, half structure and half painted illusion, that dominates the west end of the gallery.

The creation of the Long Gallery made possible a circuit of the State Rooms, almost like a connecting corridor before the concept of corridors had been invented.

The Civil War

Sir William Herbert, Sir Edward's heir, succeeded his father in 1595 and probably continued improvements to the castle. He bolstered his family's Roman Catholic credentials by marrying Eleanor Percy, daughter of the 8th Earl of Northumberland, through whom cherished relics of the martyred Mary, Queen of Scots, came to Powis in the form of a crucifix carved from bits of her bed, glass rosary beads and a fragment of textile hangings.

In 1629 Sir William was created Baron Powis by Charles I and remained loyal to the crown in the ensuing Civil War, holding the castle for the king. In the same year, Humfrey Bleaze drew a map of Powis and its estate and of the town of Welshpool. This map, which includes the earliest depiction of the castle in a thumbnail sketch, may have been drawn to record the passing of the estate from father to son because Sir Percy Herbert appears to have been in receipt of estate revenues shortly

Far Left William Herbert, 1st Lord Powis (1574–1656), English School. Depicted aged 23 in embroidered (chevron design) doublet and hose, he was created Lord Powis in 1629

Left Sir Percy Herbert, Bt, 2nd Baron Powis (c.1598–1667), English School, early 17th-century (possibly by Paul van Somer)

thereafter, long before he inherited the title from his father. If this was so, it was an arrangement with King Lear-like consequences, as father and son suffered bad relations for the rest of Lord Powis's life, Sir William even accusing Percy of treason and Percy living in self-imposed exile abroad.

On the night of 2 October 1644, a parliamentary troop under the command of Sir Thomas Myddelton of Chirk Castle advanced on Powis. Lord Powis had been preparing for this eventuality, laying up provisions for a siege. But the action was brief: 'At two of the clock even by moonlight, Mr John Arundell, the master gunner of Sir Thomas Middleton [sic], placed a petard against the outer gate which burst quite in pieces and (notwithstanding the many showers of stones) Sir T. Middleton's forces rushed with undaunted resolution into the enemy's works, got into the porch of the castle, & so stormed the castle gate, entered it & possessed themselves of the old & new Castle and of all the plate, provisions and the goods therein (which was a great store).' Lord Powis, by then an old man, was broken by the defeat and loss of his estates. He was reduced to living on £4 per week in lodgings in London, complaining in 1655 that he was '82 years old and ready to starve'. He died the following year.

The castle was occupied by 'the Welch Pool Committee' which, after due consideration, did not carry out the orders for the castle's complete demolition, contenting itself with the destruction of the outer defensive workings 'to the end that it [the castle] might thereby be made indefensible . . .'.

Percy, 2nd Lord Powis, was convicted of treason in 1651 and committed to the Tower where he wrote a philosophical treatise on his fate. He married Elizabeth Craven, sister of the romantic 1st Earl of Craven, whose love for Princess Elizabeth, sister of Charles I, was exacerbated by her fate as the exiled 'Winter Queen' of Bohemia. The earl built Ashdown House in Berkshire as a repository for the symbols of his unrequited love. Percy didn't live at Powis Castle, even after it was returned to his ownership following restoration of the monarchy in 1660, preferring a modest house at Buttington near Welshpool. It was his son William who returned to live in the castle.

'a great papist & most desperate & devilish blasphemer'

Description of the 1st Lord Powis in a parliamentary news-sheet of 1644

Left Lady Eleanor Percy, afterwards Lady Powis (1582/3–1650), aged 13, English School. The daughter of Henry Percy, 8th Earl of Northumberland, and wife of Sir William Herbert wears a brocade stomacher, full red skirt lace ruff and holds a fan

Below Carved wooden rosary traditionally associated with Mary, Queen of Scots

A Baroque Transformation

'Next is ... the (titular) duke of Powys ... represented in his great wig and robe.'

Thomas Pennant, *A tour in Wales*, 1778

William Herbert had an even more eventful career than either his father or his grandfather. He was created Earl of Powis by Charles II in 1674 but four years later was implicated in the infamous and entirely fabricated Popish Plot to replace Charles on the throne with his Roman Catholic brother James.

William, who retained his family's loyalty to Catholicism, spent five years under arrest in the Tower, missing the state progress through Wales in 1684 of his brother-in-law, the 1st Duke of Beaufort. Thomas Dineley, accompanying the Duke, left a record in sketches and descriptions of the improvements, which William had begun almost as soon as he inherited Powis in 1667. Perhaps encouraged by his opulent brother-in-law, William created a palatial state apartment comprising what is now the Blue Drawing Room, the Library and, at the opposite end of the Long Gallery, the State Bedroom. To mark receiving an earldom in 1674, William created the Grand Staircase with his earl's coronet on the ceiling. The allegorical ceiling painting, probably by the workshop of Antonio Verrio (see page 24), is thought to celebrate Charles II's Catholic queen, Catherine of Braganza. It is a very early example in Britain of this ambitious form of illusionistic painting.

Possibly a bit earlier, William had started work in the west courtyard, making good the destruction wrought by the 'Welch Committee'; a date plaque for 1668 survives. Here he created a classical entrance portico to the castle and a similar one on the east front, while building stylish and quite modest accommodation for horses and carriages. This had a terrace on the flat roof which extended along the south side of the court, giving views over his other great creation, the terraced gardens. In both of these, French taste is apparent. The hanging gardens of the terraces

Left William Herbert, 3rd Baron & 1st Earl and Marquess/Duke of Powis (1626–96), in Garter robes by François de Troy (1645–1730)

Below Lady Elizabeth Somerset, Countess of Powis (c.1633–91) by John Michael Wright (1617–94), c.1674

Left The entrance to the east-gate tower is a Jacobean composition in ashlar with four engaged Doric columns and niches for restored statues of the Saxon kings Offa and Edgar. Restoration work on the façade was completed in 2017

Below left The château of Saint-Germain-en-Laye which Louis XIV lent to the exiled court of James II. Jacobites remained there until the French Revolution. Engraving by Israel Silvestre the Younger (1621–91)

and the conceit of a roof-top terrace both appear in French prints of the period. The architect William Winde, who designed a new London house for William after the old one was burned down by a mob, seems to have been instrumental in the design of the garden terraces too. He may also have been involved with the Grand Staircase.

Life in exile

Restored to favour in 1685 on the accession of James II and made a member of the Privy Council, William is credited with trying to curb his royal master's tactless enthusiasm for Roman Catholics in public life. Unfortunately his advice went unheeded and he followed James into exile when the Glorious Revolution of 1688 placed the king's daughter, Mary, and her Protestant husband, William of Orange, on the throne. An angry mob ransacked Powis Castle after his flight; a marquessate in 1687 and a dukedom in 1689 were small compensation for this and exile in France.

At Saint Germain-en-Laye, the palace Louis XIV lent James for his court in exile, William was appointed Comptroller of the Royal Household while his wife was governess of the royal children. Portraits of great sophistication by François de Troy date from this period and now hang at Powis. William died in exile in 1696, lamented by James's queen, Mary of Modena: 'My partner has lost a most honest, zealous servant; and I a most faithful friend.'

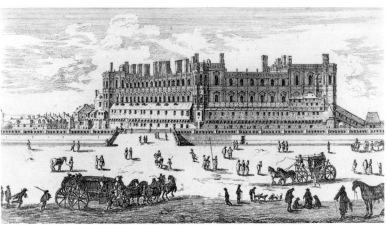

The Blue Drawing Room

'In one ceiling is much incense to the ladies of the family …'

Thomas Pennant,
A tour in Wales, 1778

At the head of the stairs, in the place where Sir Edward Herbert had his Elizabethan Great Chamber, is the Blue Drawing Room. Its blue-green panelling picked out in gold is very much in the taste of the 1930s when Guy Dawber redecorated it for the 4th Earl of Powis. Otherwise it has changed very little since 1705 when Gerard Lanscroon, a follower of Antonio Verrio (the decorative painter most likely to have created the Staircase ceiling) was commissioned to paint the allegory of *Peace banishing War from the Four Continents* on the ceiling.

Its evolution from a Great Chamber where Elizabethan society ate, drank and were entertained to today's drawing room encompassed a period as a dining room towards the end of the 18th century.

Much of the furniture in the state apartment now can be traced to the Clive family whose inheritance of Powis in the early 19th century brought many Asian and other fashionable items to the tired old castle. Its neglect in the later 18th century had aroused the censure and disgust of diarists and visitors. The fabulous pair of commodes (cupboards) is made of panels of Chinese lacquer, imported in sheets and made into European furniture. A perfect example of curvilinear French design, these were made by Pierre Langlois, who had a shop in London selling French designs. The cast ormolu (gilt brass) mounts are especially fine. Further very fine lacquer pieces are the pair of knife boxes and the two dressing boxes (on

Right One of the Pierre Langlois commodes

Below right The Library bookcases date from 1841–2

Below The Blue Drawing Room

The Library

The Library next door is a small wedge-shaped room conceived as a turning point in the parade of the state apartment. Its ceiling by Lanscroon (dating from the 2nd Marquess's time) is crucial as it makes you turn from your passage out of the Blue Drawing Room to see the image in the correct orientation, leaving you well placed to find the door into the Oak Drawing Room without fully realising the change of direction. Pennant thought the ceiling emanated 'much incense to the ladies of the family' and depicts the four daughters of the 2nd Marquess as Virtues. Lady Mary Herbert belied her depiction as Minerva by displaying such a catastrophic lack of wisdom that her financial speculations brought the family to the brink of ruin (see page 23).

English stands) which are recorded in Clive of India's collection. The giltwood seat furniture, covered by G. F. Bodley in a damask by Watts & Co. called 'Memlinc' used to be in the Clives' London house.

The tapestries belonged to an earlier generation and were probably supplied to the 1st or 2nd Marquess. They illustrate incidents from the life of Julius Caesar and were made in Brussels. They were fixed to the wall and the panelling fitted around them.

The silver sconces bear the arms of the 2nd Marquess, but are copies made in 1904. The original set was made in 1710 by John Boddington in London. Two of these are in the National Museum of Wales in Cardiff.

The State Bedroom

The State Bedroom at Powis Castle is one of the few in Britain to retain the formal layout of a bed alcove set behind a railing. This derives from French examples, particularly at Versailles which was the epicentre of European culture to which any nobleman aspiring to be at the height of fashion would turn for inspiration.

It was created to accommodate a royal visit and was the climax of the state apartment which was laid out as a series of reception rooms leading to it. That it had to wait until the 20th century for a royal occupant is not unusual – few state bedrooms were visited by the monarch for whom they were intended. Its predominant character is baroque which suggests a date in the 1660s or 70s. The entwined 'Cs' are for King Charles, but whether they commemorate a visit by Charles I early in the Civil War or celebrate his son after the restoration of the monarchy in 1660 it is difficult to say – perhaps it is both. Elements of the decoration are decidedly old-fashioned for such an advanced and cosmopolitan design – the form of the panelling and the diamond-carved pedestals of the columns are Jacobean in character, more suited to the pre-Civil War era. This suggests the decoration of the room may have taken several decades.

William, the 1st Marquess, lived at the castle before he succeeded his father in 1667. Whilst he recorded his work on the stables with a date plaque for 1668, it seems unlikely that he started restoration of the castle on a project so relatively mundane. Is it not more likely that he

'At the end of this Gallery is a pleasant Bed-chamber, with alcove, … the furniture is of Crimson velvet … ye Ballastars are also richly guilded and deversify'd.'

Thomas Dineley, *The Account of the Official Progress of His Grace Henry, the First Duke of Beaufort through Wales in 1684*'

began work on a state bedroom early in the 1660s, using local craftsmen from Shrewsbury? Their struggles with the new baroque forms of bountiful swags and flowing ribbons are evident in the frieze above the bed alcove, which appears stiff and lifeless when compared with the work of the more accomplished designers and craftsmen commissioned later to produce the alcove details and the rail (the balusters are similar to those on the stairs).

The lack of documentary evidence makes it impossible to be sure, but it seems very likely that William was working on his state apartment (the Blue Drawing Room shares cornice and panelling details with the State Bedroom) long before he achieved his earldom in 1674 and commissioned the first of the great decorative paintings in the castle. Whatever the truth of the matter, the wholly French (and thus suspiciously Catholic) guiding spirit that oversaw the planning of the state apartment – from the Bedroom, with its bed alcove, to the grand circuit of state rooms shoe-horned into the rhomboid floorplan of the medieval keep – suggests the inspiration of someone imbued with continental style and taste, someone just like William, 1st Marquess of Powis.

Grand furnishings

The possession of gilded furniture, richly upholstered, was a sign of aristocratic wealth and status. Royalty asserted itself with silver furniture (furniture with patterns embossed in silver veneered over it). Those who would aspire to have royalty visit them might equip themselves with silvered furniture – furniture covered in silver leaf – as a rare and costly alternative to gilding. The silvered seat furniture here probably started life in the Powis's town house. Now upholstered in the richest of crimson silk cut-velvets to match the rococo bed, it makes a suitably royal statement in this grandest of State Bedrooms.

Left The state bed of partly gilded mahogany is covered with crimson Spitalfields silk cut-velvet of c.1725, but only the inside of the canopy appears to be of this date. The frame, posts and gilt cresting are c.1780

Right A Boulle bracket clock stands on a French commode of c.1690 decorated with elaborate marquetry and ormolu mounts

The Baroque garden

Humfrey Bleaze details gardens to the south of the castle in his map of 1629 but only two ranks of terracing appear below the west court. These terraces are an obvious refinement of the natural topography of the castle mount where it shelves away to form the valley to the south.

Their grand realisation was William Herbert's, in the years before his exile. The practical knowledge of engineering required to create the terraces and the spectacular waterworks was probably supplied by William Winde whose experience as a military engineer would have suited him to the task.

Below *A Perspective View of Powes* [sic] *Castle in the County of Montgomery* by Samuel and Nathaniel Buck, 1742

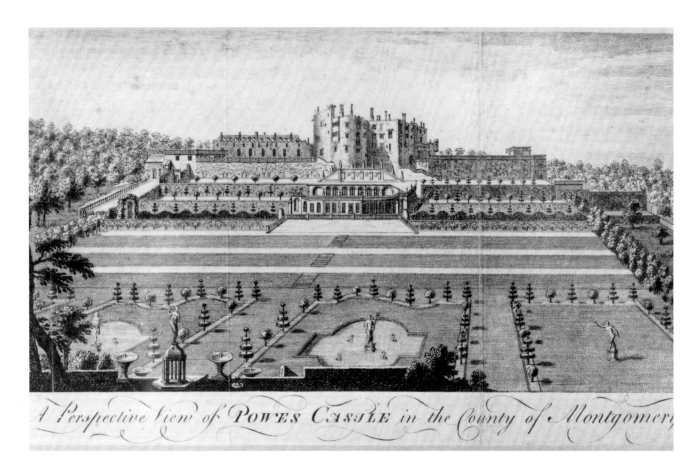

A Perspective View of POWES CASTLE in the County of Montgomery

'… the waterworks and fountains … are much beyond anything I ever saw whose streams play near twenty yards in height.'

John Bridgeman writing to his father in 1705

Winde was rebuilding the 1st Marquess's London house in 1684–7 so it is natural that he would have been asked to advise at Powis. Some waterworks were in evidence as early as 1684 when Thomas Dineley records a fountain playing in the west courtyard. William's flight in 1688 paused works, and when the Marchioness returned in 1703 she brought with her a French gardener, Adrian Duval, who stayed at Powis for the rest of his life and is buried in Welshpool.

An engraving of the south front of the castle by S. & N. Buck in 1742 shows the formal gardens at their zenith. An aviary and an orangery sit below the castle, one above the other on descending terraces which extend the whole length from the eastern entrance to the new stables in the west. Quantities of urns, statues (in lead, probably from the workshop of Jan van Nost) and balustrading clothe the terraces which are planted with formal arrays of trained fruit trees and toparian yews.

In the foreground below, large beds edged with topiary enclose statuary and pools in which played the great fountains that so impressed the Warwickshire landowner John Bridgeman. Invisible in the engraving, but undoubtedly present because it impressed so many subsequent visitors, is a cascade which fell down the southern slope in a series of lead cisterns, ending in a 'noble Bason'. The Wilderness, a series of wooded walks in formal arrangement, lies, also out of sight and behind the artist, to the left (west).

It must have been a spectacular garden, designed to set off the great baroque palace that William was creating in the old castle. Through a combination of neglect and changes in fashion, the waterworks lasted barely a century. The terraces and Wilderness, however, despite suffering similar neglect towards the end of the 18th century, survived to be revived and replanted, notably by the 4th Countess of Powis in the early 20th century. They stand as one of the finest examples of their type in Britain. Many similar features elsewhere succumbed to the mid-18th-century fashion for the 'naturalised' landscapes of designers such as 'Capability' Brown, so it is fortunate that Powis did not. As Colt Hoare remarked in 1799, 'I regret that the modern taste of gardening has entirely put the old mode of laying our grounds out of countenance, for certainly it has great dignity of character…[and]…is the only one fit for Powys Castle'.

Above Stalls in the stables built in 1668

Below The third-level Orangery supports the second-terrace balustrade, which is decorated with four Baroque dancing figures of shepherds and shepherdesses

Politics, plenty and penury: the 2nd Marquess of Powis

William, 2nd Marquess of Powis grew up in the gilded cage of exile at Saint Germain-en-Laye. He quarrelled with his sisters over their father's will, couldn't get on with his heir and fell out with his wife to such a degree that he avoided staying with her. And despite mythologising his daughters' virtues in allegory, one led her sisters and family to financial disaster.

Nevertheless William made great efforts to continue his father's great project at Powis, despite losing part of his inheritance to another relative. The decades following his father's death in 1696 were clouded by uncertainty. Lord Rochford, to whom William III gave the confiscated Herbert estates, never lived at Powis but fought the Marquess through the courts for the right even to receive income from the Powis estates. Through a combination of leases and trusts set up before his flight to France, the 1st Marquess had so efficiently tied everything up that it proved impossible for Rochford to exact much from his royal bounty.

Furthermore, the 2nd Marquess and his Marchioness travelled to and from the Continent with a degree of freedom that must have had royal sanction, taking into account his father's conviction for treason. At the accession of Queen Anne in 1703, William and his wife seem to have returned to England for good, although the conviction was not lifted and the estates restored formally until 1722. As late as 1745 William's Roman Catholicism still made him an object of suspicion and he was arrested during the second Jacobite Rebellion.

'Now we are undone, the eldest son in a common gaol, the daughters unprovided for, the other son ruined. All this for Lady M.'

Lord Edward Herbert to his father in 1722

Despite this upturn, the Herberts remained indebted. Even the discovery of lead deposits at Mochnant, a manor acquired in 1725 which generated profits of £140,000 between 1725 and 1745, proved insufficient to underwrite the development of the castle and Lady Mary's disastrous financial dabbling.

Lady Mary Herbert
'I shall be the richest subject in Europe …'

Lady Mary was the eldest of the Marquess's children. She was also the most domineering, enmeshing her father and siblings in her money-making schemes. From an early age, Lady Mary's ambition was to escape the poverty she had known in exile. Initially she succeeded, making a fortune (on paper) on the Paris stock market, investing in the French equivalent of the South Sea Company. The Mississippi Company came to the same spectacular end in 1720 when the financial bubble burst. Not only was Lady Mary ruined, but her family who had stood surety for her loans, was forced to mortgage and to sell property.

The bailiffs moved into Powis House in London, and the 2nd Marquess spent time in a Paris prison to avoid creditors. Suing and counter-suing kept lawyers busy. Lady Mary fled with her aunt and her business partner, Joseph Gage, pursued by creditors, to Spain. Here, using her family's experience of mining she pitched to reopen disused gold mines. This proved a greater saga than Paris, with pleas to both Pretender and Pope for an even grander title (she styled herself Duquessa de Powis anyway) and costly legal cases over rights in the Andalucian mines. She pleaded with her father for more money and skilled miners. Joseph Gage, an adventurer out of the same mould as Lady Mary, longed to marry his aristocratic partner, but she prevaricated and he died, unwed and in poverty in Paris, while she moved on to meddle in family affairs once more in the succession to her childless elder brother, the 3rd Marquess, at Powis.

Below Powis House was an 18th-century building on the north side of Great Ormond Street, Bloomsbury, London. The 2nd Earl preferred to live here rather than at Powis Castle

Embellishing the palace

Despite all his woes, the 2nd Marquess continued his father's work completing the terraced gardens and state apartment of the castle. As early as 1704 Gerard Lanscroon, a follower of the decorative painter Antonio Verrio, was employed at the castle, decorating the walls of the Great Staircase and the ceilings of the Blue Drawing Room and Library.

The painting of the Great Staircase walls, featuring classical gods and goddesses, is dated 1705. Above the antics of Venus and Vulcan, the Marquess's monogram appears adorned by a ducal coronet; although unrecognised officially, locally Lord Powis was styled 'Duke' and no doubt hoped to have the dukedom confirmed. In this he was to be disappointed.

The great broadsword hanging between the doors on the landing is traditionally associated with the Lords President of the Council of Wales, who held court in Ludlow Castle during Tudor and Stuart times. The lease of Ludlow Castle was acquired from the Crown by the Herberts who purchased the freehold in 1811.

Roman treasures

On the landing of the Great Staircase is one of the classical treasures of Powis, a marble statue of a Roman Muse sitting on an altar, as if made for each other. However, these trophies of Clive of India's Grand Tour in 1774 were put together by a restorer in the 18th century. The altar of c.AD 100 is a funerary memorial to Marcus Caecilius Rufus. A ewer (jug) was traditionally carved on funerary altars, as here on one side.

'The newest article seems the painted staircase,
which is a handsome one; … the style of it is good;'

Sir John Cullum, *Journal of a Tour by Rev. Sir John Cullum through
Several Counties of England and Part of North Wales, 1774–5*

Below the stairs and on the soffit Lanscroon adopted a monochromatic painting style known as *grisaille* in imitation of stone and marble to show statues of Roman deities in niches, a bacchic procession and putti frolicking in garlands on the walls. Up on the landing, the great voluted doorcases, around which Lanscroon's illusionistic flowers and *ignudi* (nudes) drape themselves, probably date from the 1st Marquess's time when William Winde was advising. Lanscroon's work was largely overseen by the Marchioness who had returned to Powis by 1703.

A finishing touch to the terraces outside was the so-called Marquess Gate which marks the transition from park to garden at the foot of the great flight of steps on the eastern approach to the castle. An invoice in 1707 suggests that a 'Mr Willis', who was paid £30 in that year 'for a pair of Iron Gates', might have been responsible for the decorative wrought iron, of extremely high quality.

Further improvements saw the current Ballroom range joined to the keep by a new wing containing further state rooms, but these were burnt to the ground in 1727 and not replaced until 30 years later.

Above The ceiling painting of the Grand Staircase was commissioned by the 1st Marquess from Antonio Verrio (c.1639–97) who came to England in 1672. It is based on a painting by Veronese in the Doge's Palace in Venice and may be intended to represent the coronation of Charles II's queen, Catherine of Braganza

A new creation

William, the 3rd Marquess was a 47-year-old bachelor, broken by the machinations of his elder sister, by the time he inherited Powis in 1745. He turned to drink and an early grave in 1748. Hardly on speaking terms with any of his immediate family, he left the estates to his Protestant ninth cousin Henry, Lord Herbert of Chirbury, of Oakly Park near Ludlow.

Immediately his meddling sister Lady Mary interfered on behalf of her niece, Barbara, who had been passed over in this partisan will. Henry, a 48-year-old bachelor, quelled the burgeoning legal battle by proposing marriage to the 16-year-old Barbara. In 1751 they were married and had two children in what was (largely) a happy 21-year union.

On inheriting, Henry petitioned for the revival of the ancient Herbert titles, as the 3rd Marquess had hoped he would, and was rewarded with the re-creation of the Powis earldom as 1st Earl of the second creation. Financial woes, however, continued to dog the family. Barbara, the new countess, took after her aunt in loving to gamble, while Henry was a leading player in the local Whig aristocracy in Shropshire with all the attendant costs, bribes and backhanders that 18th-century electioneering entailed. Even after selling the Hendon and Northamptonshire estates, Lord Powis reckoned he still owed the staggering sum of £306,175 8s 4d.

The couple lived at Oakly Park in preference to Powis, despite Sir George Lyttleton's astonishment: 'were I in the place of Lord Powis, I should forsake Okeley park … and fix my seat there [at Powis], as most eligible in every respect.' This didn't mean that Lord Powis neglected his inheritance entirely. During the decade of the 1750s he instructed the local architect William Baker to undertake work at Oakly and, at the same time, the Powis wing burnt in 1727 was

Left William Herbert, 3rd Marquess of Powis (c.1698–1748), Continental School

Right Henry Arthur Herbert, 1st Earl of Powis (second creation) (1703–72), attributed to Thomas Hudson (1701–79), c.1740. As a loyal Protestant who had raised a regiment to oppose the Jacobite uprising of Bonnie Prince Charlie, the 1st Earl was well placed to persuade George II to revive the Powis peerage

'… its walls and towers are heavy; and its neglected and languishing state still farther subducts from its picturesque effect.'

Henry Skrine, *Two successive tours throughout the whole of Wales*, 1798

POWIS CASTLE, *in* MONTGOMERYSHIRE.

was partly rebuilt as domestic offices with a Great Kitchen. It seems highly likely that Baker oversaw this work for Lord Powis.

In 1771 the rising tide of debt caught up with Henry and Barbara, and Oakly Park had to be sold. The purchaser was the head of an ancient Shropshire family and national hero of the hour, Robert Clive, Lord Clive of India. This contact between the two families prefigured a far greater and more momentous connection that was to be made in the next generation.

After considering construction of a new house in the ruins of Ludlow Castle, the earl settled on a move to Powis, and a survey of the castle, by now quite dilapidated, was commissioned. The architect selected was Thomas Farnolls Pritchard of Shrewsbury, but before his survey could be acted on, Lord Powis died leaving a 17-year-old heir.

Above An engraving of a dilapidated Powis

A Roman holiday

As the wealthy if indebted heir to an ancient earldom, George, 2nd Earl of Powis had two duties in life; one was to marry and beget an heir, and the other was to go on a Grand Tour of the cultural hotspots of Europe.

He failed in the former but succeeded spectacularly in the latter, spending the year of 1775–6 in Rome where he had his portrait painted by Pompeo Batoni (obligatory for all

milordi on the Grand Tour) and gathered exquisite works of antiquity and of more recent times. These he brought back to Powis in triumph, where he celebrated his coming of age with a grand ball in his newly constructed Ballroom.

The greatest of his purchases, possibly, is the Roman *pietra dura* table slab in the Long Gallery, made up in a jigsaw of semi-precious stones and marbles. It rests on its original Renaissance

Below George Edward Henry Arthur Herbert, 2nd Earl of Powis (1755–1801) by Pompeo Batoni (1708–87), signed and dated 1777

Below Detail of *pietra dura* table, Florence or Rome, *c.*1600. The oblong marble top decorated with inlaid hardstones depicts insects, birds and flowers

frame and stand. Though such *pietra dura* masterpieces survive in other British country-house collections (Charlecote Park in Warwickshire has a splendid example) none retains its original stand. These were often carved in stone or marble and were too heavy and awkward to bring back with the table slab. The Powis stand is of carved and gilded wood and is of the greatest magnificence. The presence of little carved pears in the capitals of the columns at the back of the grotesque semi-leonine supports suggests ownership by a member of the Peretti family. One of its members was the great building Pope of the Baroque era, Sixtus V, who used three pears for his coat of arms. That the table was originally acquired in Italy by George, however, is not certain; another possible purchaser a century earlier was the Earl of Castlemaine, the brother-in-law of the 1st Marquess of Powis – the rage for *pietra dura* items in the British Isles started in the 16th century and lasted well into the 19th.

George did not marry. A friend of George III, he seems to have preferred life in London to the Marches. However, Torrington's cruel judgement of him does not ring entirely true; George was an active landlord. He spent time and money preparing the grounds of Ludlow Castle for public enjoyment and actively promoted the local canal networks in Shropshire and Montgomeryshire to the benefit of his tenantry. In his will of 1799 he directed his trustees to keep 'Powis Castle ... in the most complete and Perfect state of Repair' and stressed that his eventual heir should 'make Powis Castle his or her principal residence'.

This heir was to be his nephew, Edward, the son of his sister Henrietta who had married Edward Clive, 2nd Lord Clive, the son of 'the conqueror of India' in 1784. Edward changed his name to Herbert in accordance with his uncle's will after he came of age and inherited Powis in 1807.

Left The table is supported on two arches and six decorated Ionic columns above a solid base. The plinth to the table has six carved and giltwood figures with human torsos terminating in single lion foot and scroll, with lion heads at the corners and lionesses at the centre

'The present (grandly descended) peer is a mean, silly man, and the bubble of his mistress ... who rarely comes here to sneak for about a day or two'

Lord Torrington, *A Tour to North Wales*, 1784

The castle surveyed

Thomas Farnolls Pritchard (c.1723–77) was the first architect to design successfully in cast iron. The elegant bridge spanning the valley at Coalbrookdale, a key structure of the early Industrial Revolution, was the product of Pritchard's final years.

Adept at designing in the Gothick and Rococo tastes (as at Croft Castle) and latterly in the new forms of Neo-classicism, Pritchard was pre-eminent in Shropshire for his main practice in country houses and churches. Lord Powis's patronage at Oakly and later at Ludlow made Pritchard the obvious choice to undertake a survey of Powis when circumstances forced the Earl and Countess to live in the old castle and make it into a modern home.

The castle was in poor repair; visitors in the later 18th century reported its uncared-for state, although few were as damning as Lord Torrington who declared in 1784: 'It is built around a court…is sadly neglected, and hourly falling to decay…not even the fruit is attended to; the ballustrades and terraces are falling down and the horses graze on the parterres!!!'

Pritchard expressed concern about the state of the roof, the copings and windows, although admitting 'that the outside walls stand upright and well'. In the interior Pritchard recorded the (by then) venerable decorations of the state apartment, noting that 'the whole … Apartment makes a Noble Antique Appearance, and ought to be preserved nearly in the present state'. However, he castigated the failure of the current arrangement to take full advantage of the splendid views over the gardens, a legacy of the castle's medieval origins: 'It is particularly to

'The whole … has a most elegant appearance, and shou'd be preserved to keep up the Stile and Dignity of the Old Castle.'

T.F. Pritchard, *A Description of the Present State of Powis Castle,* 1772

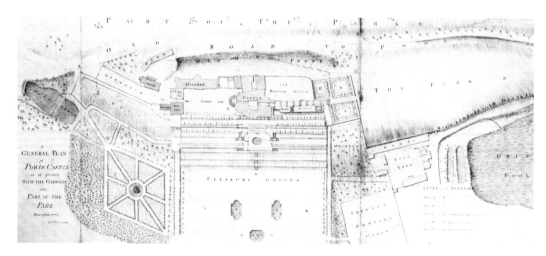

Left Thomas Farnolls Pritchard's survey plan of Powis Castle and Gardens, 1771

Right The Ballroom, showing the entrance underneath the musicians' gallery. The gallery is supported on attenuated columns which were a Pritchard hallmark

Below right The Ballroom bookcases of inlaid mahogany came from Clive of India's house, Walcot Hall in Shropshire, in 1929

be remarked….that all the South side…whence there is a fine view of the most beautiful landscape, the rooms…are low and of small dimentions, …and not at all suitable to the dignity of this ancient structure and the uncommon fine prospect it commands.'

Work began on some of Pritchard's proposals, but the death of Henry, 1st Earl in September 1772 called a halt. When work resumed (at an estimated £10,000), the only major improvement to be completed seems to have been the Ballroom in the old north wing in the west court. Here Pritchard created a Neo-classical apartment out of a derelict space. It was elegantly fitted up with fashionable Neo-classical ornament in plaster and wood and punctuated by colonnades, but awkwardly proportioned as the long narrow form of the building dictated.

Nothing further in Pritchard's ambitious designs for more bedrooms and better domestic quarters seems to have been achieved. The 2nd Earl marked his coming-of-age in his new Ballroom in 1776 and then left Powis largely to its own devices. Eight years later Lord Torrington thought it 'grievous to see the devastation that long neglect and late winds have committed on this place; as some great windows are quite forc'd in, and the hangings are waving in the air!' Perhaps the £10,000 price tag for Pritchard's plans put off the young earl, or more likely his financially cautious agent, Probert. Nevertheless when George died in 1801, there was still a debt of £177,000 against the estate.

The 19th Century

Edward Clive was the son of Robert Clive, the great general and tactician who defeated the French in India, securing British dominance over the subcontinent. In recognition of his outstanding service, Robert was created Lord Clive of Plassey (named after his greatest victory over the French). Edward followed his father into the service of the East India Company, becoming Governor of Madras in 1798 and taking his wife and two daughters out there to live with him.

'... it seemed impossible there shou'd be a great victory in this Country without a Clive being concerned in it.'

Lord Mornington to Henrietta Antonia, Lady Clive 4 June, 1799

In 1801 his son, another Edward, inherited Powis and all its estates from his maternal uncle, the childless George, 2nd Earl of Powis. Edward was still a minor, so the management of the estates fell to his father and mother. In 1804 Edward, Lord Clive was created 1st Earl of Powis (of the third creation) in recognition of his work in India and of his son's inheritance.

The turn of the century was a turbulent time in British India. The Governor of Madras – in effect second-in-command in India – took responsibility for the entire southern part of the subcontinent in which the native kingdom of Mysore remained the last serious opponent to British supremacy. Its ruler, Tipu Sultan, the son of a usurper who had taken the French side in the recent wars, was finally defeated in the last of a series of battles against the British in 1799. The campaign was led by Lord Mornington, the Company's Governor-General in Calcutta, supported by the newly arrived Lord Clive.

Left Portrait miniature of Robert Clive, 1st Baron Clive of Plassey ('Clive of India'), (1725–74) after Sir Nathaniel Dance-Holland by John Smart I (1741–1811), 1778

A remarkable expedition

In the aftermath of the victory over Tipu Sultan and the capture of his capital at Seringapatam, Henrietta, Countess of Powis undertook an extraordinary journey in March 1800. With a baggage train consisting of 14 elephants, 2 camels and about 750 attendants and soldiers, she set out on a 1,000-mile expedition into the heart of the recently conquered territory, accompanied by her two daughters and their governess (and skilled artist) Anna Tonelli. Her husband's duties kept him in Madras.

The progress, with almost royal pomp, had political as well as cultural significance. The projection of British power in Mysore was achieved through diplomacy in the exchange of gifts between Henrietta and the restored Rajah (and his grandmother). Art, both collected on the journey and created by Anna Tonelli (some of which were intended for reproduction and dissemination around the world), fulfilled a similar purpose. These included a posthumous portrait of Tipu on his fabled golden throne. Small parts of the throne were presented to Henrietta as the trophies of war. Other presentations, of jewels and gold, had to be diplomatically declined, but less valuable items – textiles, shells, armour, minerals and botanical

specimens were acceptable, and the prize of Tipu's extraordinary tent and 'the bed made for Tippoo' were also secured. These, together with Clive of India's collection, formed the nucleus of what was later to become the Clive Collection at Powis Castle. Tipu's Arab mare, Sultana, came to Powis too.

The new earl's management of his son's inheritance was so efficient and well planned that it eliminated the debt inherited with the estate and nearly doubled annual income. On coming-of-age in 1807, Edward Clive changed his name to Herbert and assumed the courtesy title of Viscount Clive until he succeeded his father as 2nd Earl of Powis in 1839. He also took over the management of the Powis estates and came to live at the castle.

Left A wall panel from Tipu Sultan's tent, later Mughal decoration, c.1725–50. Cotton chintz with a white ground, patterned with acanthus cusped niches, each enclosing a central vase with symmetrical flower arrangement

Below Lady Henrietta Herbert, Countess of Powis (1758–1830) by Sir Joshua Reynolds (1723–92), 1777–8

The Clive Collection

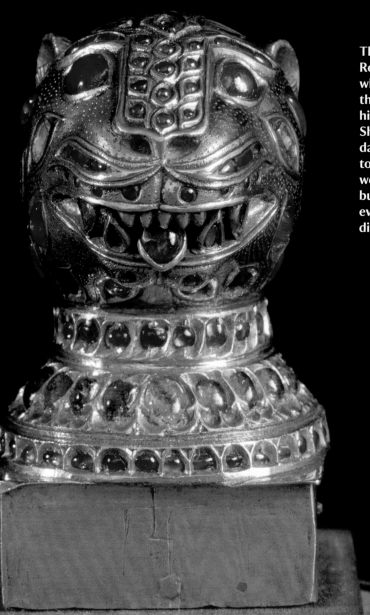

The collection consists of items amassed by Robert, Lord Clive of Plassey, 'Clive of India', which were housed originally at Claremont, the suburban villa Lord Clive built for himself south of London and at Oakly Park in Shropshire. The collections of his son and daughter-in-law derived from their time together in Madras. Initially, these treasures were kept at Walcot, their Shropshire home, but upon their son's coming of age in 1806, everything was brought to Powis for formal display in the Ballroom.

'… a sort of museum of curiosities brought from India by the great Lord Clive'

Cambrian Mirror, 1846

The collection spans Indian and other Eastern decorative arts, including metalwork, textiles, paintings, arms and armour, jewellery, carved woodwork, furniture and ceramics.

Some items, such as Tipu's bed, the pair of rose-water sprinklers, the bejewelled tiger head from Tipu's throne and Sèvres coffee cups were once part of the great riches of Tipu's palace in Seringapatam, which was looted and the spoils auctioned off. A far greater portion relates to Clive of India's periods of military service earlier in the century, and yet more to the collecting of his son and daughter-in-law in Madras. Portraits of native princes by both Indian and European artists – Thomas Hickey established himself in Madras during the time of Lord Clive's governorship – formed diplomatic gifts.

Botanical specimens, many of which have not survived, and minutely detailed paintings of animals and plants that inhabited menageries and herbaria, form an important record of the flora and fauna that surrounded Edward and Henrietta's Madras. Indian arms and armour were of the greatest fascination; George, 2nd Earl of Powis wrote to his brother-in-law in 1801 requesting some 'Asiatic Armour' for a display in the Ballroom. Daggers, swords, scimitars, helmets and chain mail form a major part of the collection.

Below A Sèvres saucer of 1786 from Tipu Sultan's palace. It was one of the items of porcelain given to the Mysore embassy in 1788 when it visited the factory as part of a mission to establish a trade relationship with France

Left A late 18th-century ceremonial staff (chubb) from south or east India. The ivory shaft is surmounted by a tiger's head of chased, engraved cast silver

Far left Maharaja Pratap Singh of Tanjore (1739–65). Gouache, gold and iridescent beetle wing

Opposite A tiger-head finial from the throne of Tipu Sultan who ruled from 1782 to 1799

The castle remodelled

Between 1815 and 1818, Edward, Viscount Clive employed Sir Robert Smirke, doyen of the architectural establishment and designer of the British Museum among other great national monuments, to undertake a thorough refurbishment of the castle.

Smirke's practice was largely amongst the Tory aristocracy – he provided a family mausoleum for the arch-reactionary, the 4th Duke of Newcastle, at Markham near Clumber Park in Nottinghamshire, and in 1812 he designed a complete castle in the Norman style for the 1st Earl Somers at Eastnor in Herefordshire.

Despite Pritchard's work a generation earlier, Powis had been described in 1802 as 'going fast to decay. The buildings are in a state of dilapidation', so much of Smirke's work was the mundane repair of windows, replastering and whitewashing, rebuilding chimneys and work to roofs. His removal of 'old white French sashes' met with approval from the Cambrian Archaeological Association on their visit to the castle in 1856, which noted that the replacement of them by 'the present windows [is] very much to the improvement of the Castle . .'.

Smirke left his mark on the old castle in even more tangible ways, extending the domestic wing between the Ballroom and keep to its current proportions. Most significantly, he raised the East Tower by an additional storey, transforming the appearance of the castle, emphasising the romantic irregularity of its silhouette and reinforcing its dominance over the surrounding countryside.

Lord Clive recast the ante-room between the Blue Drawing Room and the Oak Drawing Room as a Library, installing bookcases to carry his collection of early manuscripts and much of the contents of the Empress Josephine's library from Malmaison (bought at the sale after Napoleon's exile and largely sold again in 1923).

Below *Edward Herbert, 1st Lord Herbert of Cherbury* as a melancholy knight and lover, by Isaac Oliver (1565–1617)

'Powis has improved his Castle sensibly, and slowly; but he has yet a great deal to do to make it as comfortable as it is capable of being made'

Lord Palmerston, 1841, quoted in *Powis Castle, Past and Present* 1882

In the Library, later generations have gathered some of the great treasures of Powis, including two representations of the celebrated ancestor of the Herberts of Chirbury, Edward, 1st Lord Herbert of Cherbury (who uniquely used this spelling), in a bronze bust by Hubert Le Sueur and a miniature by Isaac Oliver. Both are masterpieces of their genres, the bust one of the earliest portrait bronzes in England and the miniature a representation of the epitome of courtly love, laced with allegory and laden with the romance of contemplative melancholy. Edward was a courtier, politician and poet at the courts of James I and Charles I, writing what is probably one of the first autobiographies in English.

A royal visit

In August 1832 the 13-year-old Princess Victoria visited Powis with her mother, the Duchess of Kent, as part of a tour of her future realm. This unashamed bid for popularity so infuriated her uncle, William IV, that he publicly insulted the Duchess at the state dinner in celebration of his birthday. Victoria is supposed to have slept in the State Bedroom on her visit, although it is doubtful she did so alone as the Duchess insisted on sleeping in her daughter's bedroom every night to keep a maternal eye on the young princess.

Edward succeeded his father as 2nd Earl of Powis in 1839 and enjoyed a tenure foreshortened by a shooting accident when wounds received from the accidental discharge of the gun of one of his sons proved fatal and he died in 1848.

Left Edward (Clive) Herbert, 2nd Earl of Powis (1785–1848) by Sir Francis Grant (1803–78), 1845

Below left Lady Lucy Graham, Countess of Powis (1793–1875), by Frederick Richard Say (1805–60)

The 20th Century

Edward Herbert, 3rd Earl, was a bachelor who did little to the castle during his long reign but devoted himself to scholarly works and local politics – the latter largely on a ceremonial basis (as Lord Lieutenant of Montgomeryshire) once his time as an MP was over. Disraeli's offer of the post of Viceroy of India in 1875, presumably in recognition of the family's long and illustrious association with that country, was politely declined in public but, more revealingly, on the envelope containing the offer, the Earl scribbled, 'Not worth considering'.

On his death in 1891 he was succeeded as 4th Earl by his nephew, George. In 1890 George had married Violet Lane-Fox who was that rare thing, a female peer in her own right as 16th Baroness Darcy de Knayth – a title still carried on by her great grandchildren. However, the Powis earldom did not descend to the next generation of George and Violet's children because two world wars claimed the lives of their two sons, Percy, Viscount Clive in 1916 and his younger brother, Mervyn, Viscount Clive in 1943.

In happier times, both husband and wife had confided their thoughts, plans and recollections of the castle and its gardens to notebooks. In the gardens Violet, Lady Powis, having wrested management of the whole from her reluctant husband, was determined to move the kitchen gardens away from the castle and out of sight. A greater urgency attended the scheme after storms brought down two of 'four very fine elms'. Once the remaining pair, a screen of pollarded

Left Edward James Herbert, 3rd Earl of Powis (1818–91) by Sir Francis Grant (1803–78), 1845/8

elms and a beech hedge had been taken down in consequence, Lady Powis declared herself 'aghast at the havoc caused – and distressed at the cruel eyesore [of] the kitchen garden in its bareness and in all its tastelessness [exposed to]…. the terraces. I soon decided that, since mighty elms cannot be commanded, the only thing to do was to remove the eyesore.'

Sacrifices had to be made: 'I have cut down seven hideous sordid little buildings… In there sheltered all the hot house flowers…but surely it is better to have no hot house flowers than to be greeted every day by the repulsive sight of the detestable little houses', and slowly the kitchen gardens were removed to their new location. They were replaced by a formal garden with 'wide paths: rose gardens, fountains, clipped yews, marble seats, herbaceous borders, What not!' Violet had a pair of wrought-iron gates 'with a little gold on them' made for her husband's next '(and many future) birthdays' in 1912. These were designed by the great architect and designer G.F. Bodley who had been retained by her husband to undertake the last and possibly the most thoroughgoing restoration to which the castle had ever been subjected.

Top left George Herbert, 4th Earl of Powis (1862–1952) by Walter Stoneman, 1925. Stoneman photographed over 7,000 prominent members of British society for the National Portrait Gallery

Top right Violet, Countess of Powis (1865–1929) by Ellis Roberts (1860–1930)

Right The Bodley gates with the Powis coat of arms, combining the elephant of the Clives with the griffon of the Herberts and a wyvern surmounting each pillar

G.F. Bodley and revival

George, 4th Lord Powis engaged the celebrated architect G. F. Bodley to make proposals, first to rationalise the layout of rooms on the north front of the ground floor and later to advise on the refurbishment of bedrooms and the Oak Drawing Room upstairs. This coincided with the introduction of electricity to the castle for the first time and a new heating system.

Bodley, who was coming towards the end of an illustrious career as a church and country-house architect, was known to Lord Powis through his involvement with the design of his cousins' house at Hewell Grange in Worcestershire. George was also impressed by the sensitivity of the architect's work at Ham House in Surrey.

It is striking how much Lord Powis was involved in the detail of the work. The State Dining Room was created out of a bedroom and some smaller service rooms. At his suggestion new panelling was copied from a 16th-century fragment discovered behind a later fireplace surround, and the fireplaces were based on one in the V&A, from the Old Palace at Bromley-by-Bow, which George 'much admired'.

George recalled the Oak Drawing Room being 'painted pale green and the ceiling was a poor one in the style of Adams'. This was probably the 'frenchify'd drawing room' Lord Torrington mentioned had been 'trick'd up' on his second visit in 1793. Smirke's elegant, early 19th-century bow window was replaced by the present large mullioned window. Bodley wrote: 'As soon as this was done, I saw that it was necessary to do the whole room in the same style.' The frieze in the Long Gallery was copied, with variations in the heraldry, and uniform panelling was introduced to a design by Bodley. The ceiling was copied from the great Jacobean mansion of Aston Hall in Birmingham, the pendants provoking much discussion between architect and client (the addition of the smaller ones was George's idea). Fragments of 16th-century plasterwork in window bays were preserved.

Right G.F. Bodley's State Dining Room viewed from the door to the Entrance Hall, 1905 by Henry Charles Brewer (1866–1950)

Far right The State Dining Room ceiling was inspired by one in the old Reindeer Inn in Banbury, Oxfordshire

'I always found Mr Bodley most willing to listen to my suggestions … and to assist me … even after I had rejected some plan or proposal of his.'

Notebook of George, 4th Earl of Powis, c.1932

Bodley was blessed with craftsmen of great skill and experience. Franklin of Deddington near Oxford was the main contractor and produced the plasterers and carvers, such as Bridgeman of Lichfield, who carved the grand chimneypiece. Stained glass was supplied by Burlison & Grylls. The superb door furniture of filigree and pierced steel has been ascribed to the goldsmiths Barkentin & Krall who also made church plate for Bodley. Watts fabrics in olive green were deployed as upholstery and curtains in the Oak Drawing Room, to counteract the 'foxy' tones of the new oak.

The Duke's Room, used as a sitting room for the countess although now shown as a bedroom, retains its Elizabethan plasterwork, but the panelling and fireplace surround are all to Bodley's design with the original Tudor fireplace reduced on Bodley's advice.

Not everything went well. The lead statue of 'Fame' was set in a fountain by Bodley, but was disparaged by the countess who declared 'the horse looked as if it was trying to jump out of a footbath – and not succeeding'. The pool was removed and the statue had to wait until the 1980s for a suitable plinth to be designed.

The Ballroom was reduced in length and given mullioned and transomed windows, much to George's delight, while the Baroque screen at the west entrance to the keep, which 'wobbled', was removed to the Orangery and the original medieval vaulting revealed.

Above The lead sculpture of 'Fame' borne aloft by the winged horse Pegasus by Andries Carpentière/ Andrew Carpenter (c.1677–1737), c.1705

The bequest of Powis

'In the main building is a small collection of antiques, some of which are supposed to be valuable'

Rev. W. Bingley, *A tour round North Wales, performed during the summer of 1798*

The tragedy of losing both heirs in the world wars was compounded for the 4th Earl by the death of the countess as a result of a car crash in 1929. Their daughter, who had married an Italian duke, and granddaughters, Violetta and Davina, through whom the Barony of Darcy de Knayth continues, were the only family left to him.

It is perhaps unsurprising therefore, with the prospect of the title and estates passing to cousins, that the 4th Earl should consider leaving Powis to the nation; on his death in 1952 at the age of 91, the castle, gardens and part of the deer park passed into the care of the National Trust.

The great Herbert and Clive collections remain in the castle. The greatest painting is by Canaletto's nephew and pupil Bernardo Bellotto whose *View of Verona* is justly famous, conveying the dreamy heat of a Veneto afternoon. It was acquired by Clive of India for his London home in Berkeley Square, and recorded for the first time at Powis in 1798 when many of Lord Clive's pictures were in the castle for safe-keeping while he was Governor of Madras. It was acquired from the Powis Estate Trustees in 1981 with the aid of the National Heritage Memorial Fund, the Art Fund and the V&A.

Among other treasures is the portrait by Reynolds of Henrietta Antonia, Countess of Powis, which holds a surprise. Almost jaunty in her parasol-hat, Henrietta is depicted at the height of fashion in 1777. A mezzotint of the portrait shows an astonishing change,

with Henrietta sporting a head-consuming chemise very much in the vogue of a decade earlier. The mezzotint will have been copied from the portrait on completion, which suggests that the portrait underwent considerable modification at a later date.

Many of Powis's tapestries were brought by the 4th Earl from an old Herbert property at Lymore during Bodley's campaign of building and decorating. After repairs directed by a lady sent by the Duke of Rutland from Haddon and undertaken by a needlewoman from Welshpool, some were hung in the Duke's Room but the reassembled great Venetian Ambassador's tapestry now hangs in the Ballroom. It is an early tapestry, dating from 1545 and important not only because of its rarity and great size, but also because it is thought to depict a real historic event when ambassadors from Venice first made diplomatic overtures to the Mamluk rulers of Damascus.

Opposite *Attack on a Fortress*, one of the three tapestries in the Blue Drawing Room by Marcus de Vos, one of the principal weavers in late 17th-century Brussels

Below Detail of the tapestry *The Reception* of an *Embassy*, probably made in the southern Netherlands or France, loosely based on a painting in the Louvre by an unknown Venetian artist, 1545

Overleaf *View of Verona from the Ponte delle Navi* by Bernardo Bellotto (1721–80), 1745–7

Powis today

'It is a beautiful building in a beautiful setting to be admired and enjoyed'

John, 8th Earl of Powis

The 5th and 6th Earls were brothers, cousins once removed of their predecessor, the 4th Earl. Neither had heirs to inherit the title, so it moved sideways once more to a further cousin whose son, John, is the current 8th Earl of Powis.

Powis is both a popular tourist attraction, bringing many visitors to the area, and a great resource for its local community with the park a popular place of resort. The gardens are justly famous as a great example of a rare formal design, set in a unique landscape, as well as a centre of horticultural excellence and expertise. Above all, they are known as a place of great beauty and peace.

The Castell Coch of the Princes of Powys, of the medieval romance of Gwenwynwyn and of Hawise, has softened with age. No longer a terrifying fortress or a shaky refuge, the Powis of today is a welcoming place, full of tremendous stories. It is a place of beauty and of wonder. The richness of its collections, accumulated by generations of Herberts and Clives, speaks of aristocratic lives of leisure and of service, of prudent management and (perhaps more often) of reckless expenditure. The castle itself, although remodelled in almost every generation, still appears as the great red pile of princely ambition that inspired generations to defend and embellish it, to protect and to refine it. Splendid upon its rock, it is steeped in the history of generations of its people.

Below Deer in snow

Opposite The drum towers and west door to the castle, with Andrew Carpenter's lead statue of Fame being borne aloft by Pegasus

About the author

Andrew Barber is a freelance historic buildings consultant, tour director and author, recently retired after 33 years as a curator for the National Trust. He directs tours for ACE Cultural Tours and has written guidebooks for Packwood House, Gunby Hall, Calke Abbey, Mr Straw's House and Canons Ashby.

Acknowledgements

This souvenir guide is deeply indebted to the guidebooks for Powis Castle that have preceded it, particularly those editions written by Christopher Rowell and Jane Gallagher. I have been fortunate in having access to the article 'A Game of Thrones in an Asiatic World: Henrietta Clive and Anna Tonelli in British India' prior to its publication, by kind permission of its author, John Chu. The 'Architectural and Archaeological Analysis of Powis Castle & Gardens' by Richard Morriss, February 2003, has been an invaluable source as have the two unpublished architectural studies of east and west fronts of the castle undertaken by Christopher Gallagher for access to which I am deeply grateful to the author.

The staff of the National Trust at Powis Castle and further afield in Wales have been most helpful, in particular Dr Elizabeth Green and Emma Thompson.

Illustrations

British Library Board. All Rights Reserved/Bridgeman Images pp.4, (left, right), 5 (bottom); Musée de la Ville de Paris, Musée Carnavalet, Paris/Bridgeman Images p.15 (bottom); Royal Commission on the Ancient and Historical Monuments of Wales p.5 (top); The National Library of Wales pp.9, 27 (bottom); National Portrait Gallery p.39 (top left); National Trust pp.7, 20, 30; National Trust Images pp.22, 33 (bottom), 38; National Trust Images/Sotheby's/National Museum of Wales p.10 (left); National Trust Images/Clare Bates pp.12 (left, right), 13 (top), 37 (bottom); National Trust Images/Mark Bolton p.21 (bottom); National Trust Images/Andrew Butler pp.8, 39 (bottom), 41, 46; National Trust Images/James Dobson pp.6, 13 (bottom), 15 (top), 16–17, 17 (top, bottom), 24, 31 (top, bottom), 39 (top right), 40–1; National Trust Images/John Hammond inside back fold out, pp.14 (left, right), 21 (top), 25, 28 (left, right), 36, 37 (top), 40, 42, 43, 44–5; National Trust/Simon Harris p.26; National Trust Images/Paul Highnam pp.10–11, 35 (right); National Trust Images/Chris Lacey p.10; National Trust/Kate Lynch p.35 (top); National Trust Images/John Millar pp.2–3, 46; National Trust Images/Erik Pelham contents, 32, 33 (top), 34, 35 (left); National Trust Images/Arnhel de Serra p.5 (top); National Trust/Charles Thomas p.23; National Trust Images/Andreas von Einsiedel pp.11, 18, 19, 29; National Trust Images/Joe Wainwright cover, back cover.

High-quality prints from the extensive and unique collections of National Trust images are available at **www.ntprints.com**

The National Trust and National Trust (Enterprises) Ltd are committed to respecting the intellectual property rights of others. Reasonable efforts have been made to contact, identify and acknowledge copyright holders where applicable. Any copyright holders who may be incorrectly acknowledges or omitted should contact us so that any required correction can be made.

Thank you for buying this guidebook. Your support helps us look after places like this.

The National Trust

The National Trust is a conservation charity founded in 1895 by three people who saw the importance of our nation's heritage and open spaces, and wanted to preserve them for everyone to enjoy. More than 120 years later, these values are still at the heart of everything the charity does.

Entirely independent of Government, the National Trust looks after around 250,000 hectares of countryside, 780 miles of coastline and hundreds of special places across England, Wales and Northern Ireland.

More than 26 million people visit every year, and together with 5.2 million members and over 61,000 volunteers, they help to support the charity in its work to care for special places for ever, for everyone.

If you would like to become a member or make a donation, please telephone 0344 800 1895 (minicom 0344 800 4410); write to National Trust, PO Box 574, Manvers, Rotherham S63 3FH; or visit our website at **www.nationaltrust.org.uk**

© 2019 National Trust

Registered charity number 205846

ISBN 978-1-84359-549-6

Written by Andrew Barber

Edited by Anthony Lambert

Picture research by Izzy Souster

Bird's-eye view by Robbie Polley

Designed by Matt Bourne

Printed by Pureprint Group, Uckfield for National Trust (Enterprises) Ltd, Heelis, Kemble Drive, Swindon, Wilts SN2 2NA on Revive Silk made from 100% recycled paper

RECYCLED
Paper made from recycled material
FSC® C022913

Opposite Detail of the brightly decorated two-wheeled Sicilian cart which is thought to have been given to Lady Hermione Herbert as a wedding gift on her marriage to Roberto Lucchesi-Palli, 11th Duke of Grazia in 1924, as the cart is thought to date from the 1920s. The sides depict scenes from the life of Roger II, King of Siciliy (1096–1154), with a stylised St George and the dragon